P9-CRK-082

Dedication

To my children Steven, Brian and Joanna, who have brought
so much joy and meaning to "my lifetime." To The Great Spirit for the
many wonderful experiences of "life" and
for the opportunities to learn what I need to learn and
to become who I am meant to become. —*DLR*

To Beth, Wolf and Teal. —*MSM*

Rice, David L., 1939-
    Lifetimes / by David L. Rice ; illustrated by Michael Maydak.—
1st ed.
    p. cm.
    SUMMARY: A selection of plants and animals of the world are
presented in order of their longevity, and each reveals a special
quality of their lifetime.
    ISBN: 1-883220-58-0 (hbk)
    ISBN: 1-883220-59-9 (pbk)

    1. Longevity—Juvenile literature. 2. Animal life spans—
Juvenile literature. 3. Plant life spans—Juvenile literature.
I. Maydak, Michael. II. Title.

QH528.5R53 1997   574.3'74
                                                   QBI96-40670

Published by Dawn Publications
P.O. Box 2010
Nevada City, CA 95959
800-545-7475
nature@dawnpub.com

Printed in China

12 11 10 9 8 7 6
First Edition

Designed by LeeAnn Brook Design

LIFETIMES

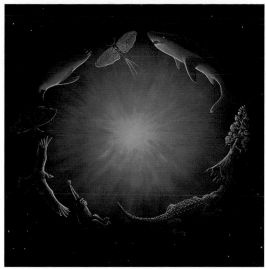

Dear fellow Earth Residents,

Our dear home, planet Earth, is having terrible problems! It's not too late
to solve them, but to do so we need to work together and respect each
species' role in Mother Nature's grand plan.

Most of us plants and animals have lived on Earth for millions of years—
far longer than humans have been around. We've learned many things
through the ages that we would like to share with your species. We hope
that after reading about our lifetimes, you will agree that:

NO MATTER HOW SHORT, NO MATTER HOW LONG,
NO MATTER HOW BIG, HOW SMART OR HOW STRONG,
ALL LIFE HAS A PLACE, A PURPOSE AND WORTH.
ALL LIFE IS IMPORTANT ON OUR PLANET EARTH.

The plants and animals
of Lifetimes

A lifetime for a **mayfly** is about **one day.**

$\mathcal{A}$dult mayflies, sometimes called "dayflies," spend most of their one day of life laying thousands of tiny eggs in the shallow water of mountain streams. If they didn't lay eggs that same day, there would be no more mayflies. When mayflies hatch, hungry trout and other fish snap them up by the hundreds. But no matter how many mayflies the fish eat, there are always enough left to lay more eggs. Mayflies have survived on Earth for over 200 million years.

Mayflies teach us that a lot can be done in just one day.

Tell about it: Tell about a time when you got a lot done in just one day.

Peabody Public Library
Columbia City, IN

Look it up: Why do some people call mayflies "dayflies"?

A lifetime for a **butterfly** is about **one month.**

As they fly from flower to flower sipping sweet nectar, butterflies brush against the pollen and carry some of it with them. By carrying pollen from flower to flower, butterflies make the seeds of plants fertile. Only fertile seeds can grow. When winter comes, all butterflies have to either migrate or hibernate. The Monarch butterfly, which lives longer than most butterflies, migrates 2,000 miles to spend the winter in Mexico. Butterflies that hibernate make a chemical a lot like the antifreeze people put in cars to keep water from freezing. This "antifreeze" keeps them alive no matter how cold it gets.

Butterflies show us it's possible to do important work and have fun at the same time.

Tell about it: Tell about a time when you helped someone do a job and had fun doing it.

Think about it: What does it mean to "have butterflies in your stomach"?

Look it up: The life cycle of a butterfly has four parts. What are they?

A lifetime for **corn** *is* **one year.**

A corn plant grows from a seed and dies at the end of every growing season. Every kernel of corn is a seed. If people did not save this seed over the winter there would be no corn crop the next year. People have been doing this without fail every year since native people in Mexico started raising corn about 5,000 years ago. Corn is such a good and abundant food that it allowed the Aztecs and Incas to live in cities and develop powerful civilizations. Columbus brought corn home to Europe with him from America and soon corn was being raised throughout Europe, Africa and Asia.

Corn reminds us to plan for the future.

Tell about it: Tell about a time when you planned ahead and everything worked out well. Or tell about a time when you didn't plan ahead and it caused you problems.

Look it up: Corn is used in hundreds of food products to make them taste or look better. It is also used in many products that are not eaten. What are some of these products?

A lifetime for an **army ant** is about **three years.**

Army ants are famous for their ability to work together to accomplish amazing things. They march along like soldiers, sometimes a million at a time. Nothing can stop them. When they come to a river, they make an "ant bridge" of themselves to get across. If the river is very wide, they form large "ant balls" and float to the other side. Army ants eat mostly insects, spiders and small animals, although they have been known to eat horses, cows and even tigers that are tied up or caged. People who live in areas with army ants have to leave their homes for a day or two when the ants come marching through. When they return their houses are completely free of rats, cockroaches, or other pests.

Army ants show us that if everyone works together, we can do almost anything.

Tell about it: Tell about a time when you were part of a group that all worked together to get a big job done.

Think about it: How do army ants know to make "ant bridges" and "ant balls"? Do you think they know what they are doing, or is it unthinking instinct?

Look it up: Where do army ants live?

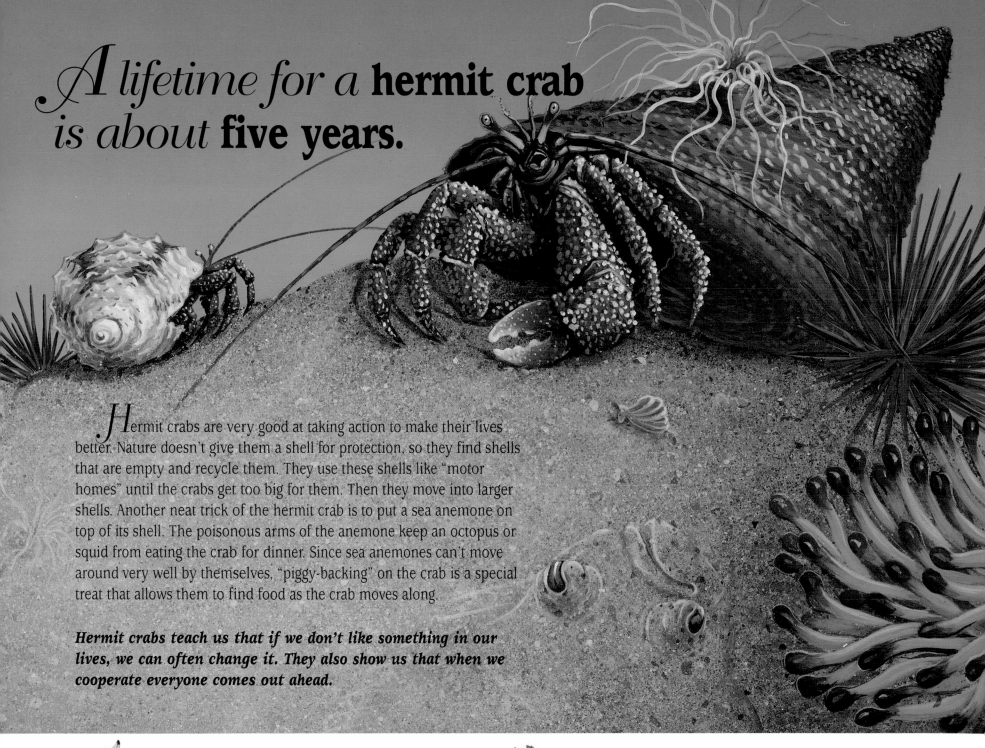

A lifetime for a **hermit crab** is about **five years.**

Hermit crabs are very good at taking action to make their lives better. Nature doesn't give them a shell for protection, so they find shells that are empty and recycle them. They use these shells like "motor homes" until the crabs get too big for them. Then they move into larger shells. Another neat trick of the hermit crab is to put a sea anemone on top of its shell. The poisonous arms of the anemone keep an octopus or squid from eating the crab for dinner. Since sea anemones can't move around very well by themselves, "piggy-backing" on the crab is a special treat that allows them to find food as the crab moves along.

Hermit crabs teach us that if we don't like something in our lives, we can often change it. They also show us that when we cooperate everyone comes out ahead.

 **Tell about it:** Tell about some times when you cooperated and everyone ended up happy.

 Think about it: How is a crab's borrowed shell like a motor home? How is it different?

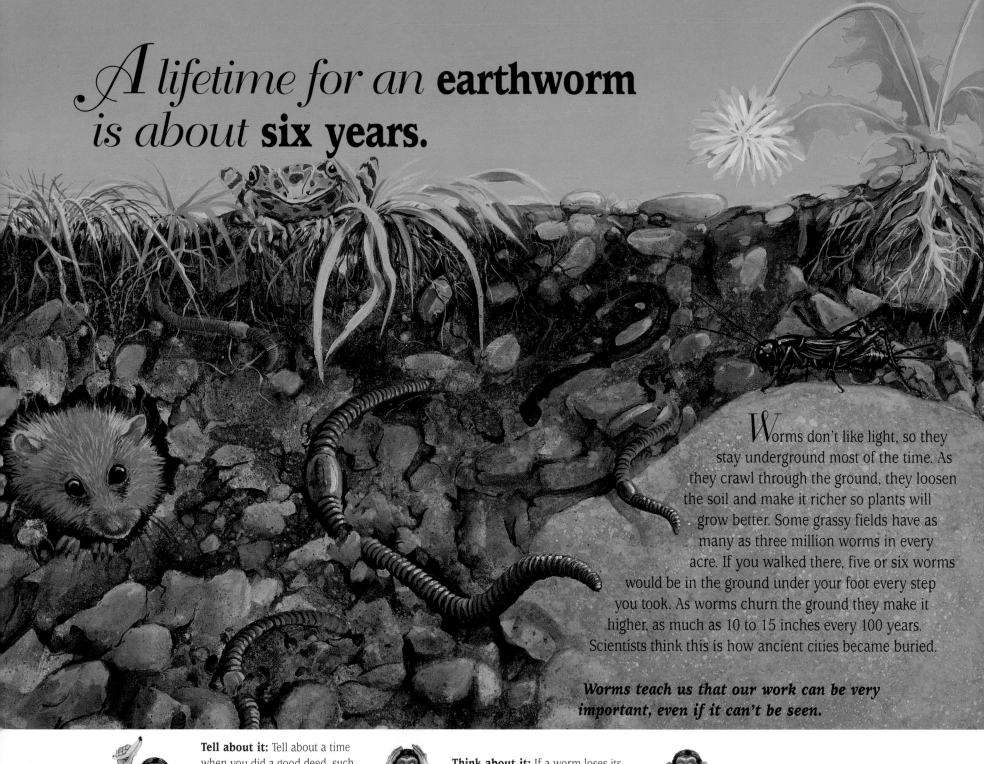

A lifetime for an **earthworm** is about **six years.**

Worms don't like light, so they stay underground most of the time. As they crawl through the ground, they loosen the soil and make it richer so plants will grow better. Some grassy fields have as many as three million worms in every acre. If you walked there, five or six worms would be in the ground under your foot every step you took. As worms churn the ground they make it higher, as much as 10 to 15 inches every 100 years. Scientists think this is how ancient cities became buried.

Worms teach us that our work can be very important, even if it can't be seen.

Tell about it: Tell about a time when you did a good deed, such as picking up trash or helping a spider or bug, and no one saw you do it.

Think about it: If a worm loses its tail, it will grow back. Will any parts of your body grow back if they get cut off or knocked out?

Look it up: Worms can tell if it is light or dark, even though they don't have eyes. How can they tell?

A lifetime for a **Venus flytrap** *is about* **18 years.**

*A*lthough most animals eat plants, the Venus flytrap is a plant that eats animals, mostly insects. At the ends of the flytrap's leaves are hair-lined traps that give off a sweet nectar smell. When an unsuspecting insect lands in the trap, expecting a treat, the trap snaps shut so fast that escape is impossible. For several days the plant digests the insect, which provides the minerals it needs. Only one small area on Earth has just the right soil and weather for the flytrap to grow. So many Venus flytraps have been dug up and sold that they are in danger of becoming extinct.

Venus flytraps remind us that things are not always as good as they first seem to be.

 Tell about it: Tell about a time when something seemed like a good idea at first, but it really wasn't.

 Think about it: Some people dig flytraps and sell them, even though it's against the law. What do you think should be done when they are caught?

 Look it up: Where is the one small area where Venus flytraps grow in the wild?

A lifetime for an **otter** is about **20 years.**

Tell about it: Tell about a day when you had a wonderful, fun time.

Think about it: What other animals have you seen playing and having fun?

Otters love to play. Some otters live in the ocean, where they jump and dive in and out of the water as they wrestle and chase each other. Other otters live in the mountains where they spend hours sliding down slippery river banks or snowy hills. Sometimes families of otters play follow the leader as they swim across a lake. Except for the leader, only the backs of the otters are above water. Some people, seeing a head followed by several humps, have thought the otters were a sea monster!

Otters show us that relaxing and having fun is an important part of life.

Look it up: Otters are mammals just like you are. Discover what makes mammals different from all other animals.

A lifetime for an Emperor Penguin is about 20 years.

*I*t takes teamwork to raise a family near the south pole. After the mother lays her egg on the ice, she walks many miles to the ocean to eat fish until she has thick layers of fat. The fat keeps her alive when there is no food to eat. During the two months she's gone, the father takes care of the egg. He carries it under a fold of skin on top of his feet to keep it warm, and never gets to eat. The mother returns just after the egg hatches, her throat full of fish for the baby. Now the father walks to the ocean to eat and get fat. When he returns, they raise the chick together.

Penguins show us how smoothly things work when mothers and fathers cooperate.

Tell about it: Tell about some special things your mother and father do for you.

Think about it: Although penguins are birds, they can't fly. They use their wings as flippers when they swim. Do you know the name of another bird that can't fly?

Look it up: Emperor penguins are the largest of all penguins. How tall are they? Are they taller or shorter than you?

A lifetime for a **shark** is about **25 years**.

Although sharks kill and eat almost any animal that comes close, there are some fish, like the pilot fish, that sharks actually help. The pilot fish swims near the shark's head for protection from its enemies, who don't want to get close to the shark. It also gets scraps from the shark's meals. No one knows why sharks don't eat pilot fish. Although most people fear them, sharks seldom bother humans. Each year sharks attack about 30 people, of whom about four die. By comparison, each year dogs bite about 600,000 people in the United States of whom about 20 die. Very few animals deliberately hurt people.

Sharks remind us that there is some good in everyone. They also remind us not to believe everything we hear about someone.

Tell about it: Tell about a time when you helped protect an animal or someone who needed help.

Think about it: Why do sharks attack people? Do they think we are going to hurt them? Do they mistake people for dolphins or some other sea animal they want to eat?

Look it up: A whale shark is the largest of all fish. It can be as long as 40 feet and weigh 3,000 pounds. How does this compare to the size of an elephant?

A lifetime for a vulture is about 35 years.

Vultures are often seen circling around and around in the sky. They soar on warm air currents rising up from the ground, seldom needing to flap their wings. As they circle, they look below for dead animals. By eating only dead and rotting animals, vultures prevent sickness and disease from spreading. One vulture, the California Condor, is one of the most endangered animals in the world. There are only about 60 left alive. If they die, the California Condor will be extinct—gone forever.

Vultures remind us that it's important to clean up messes.

Tell about it: Tell about some yucky messes you have helped clean up.

Find out: Some vultures have wing spans of 8 feet. How long is your "arm span"—from finger tip to finger tip? Is this distance longer or shorter than your height?

Look it up: What is being done to keep the California Condor from becoming extinct?

A lifetime for a **chimpanzee** *is about* **40 years.**

Chimpanzees are more like people than any other animal. They are very intelligent, and are one of only a few animals who can make and use tools. For example, they use stones to crack nuts and leaves to wipe their sticky hands. Some chimps have even been taught to use computers and to understand and use words. Mothers carry their babies and take care of them for several years. Young chimps are very obedient and almost always do what their mothers tell them. If a chimp doesn't obey it's mother, do you think she tells it to stop acting like a human?

Chimpanzees remind us that we may not be as different from the animal kingdom as we sometimes think we are.

 Tell about it: Many animals are intelligent. Tell about some things you have seen a dog, cat, or other animal do that shows they are smart.

 Think about it: A tool can be anything you use to help do something. What are some tools you use almost every day?

 Look it up: Chimpanzees are apes, not monkeys. There are three other kinds of apes. Find out what they are.

A lifetime for a **whale** is about **45 years.**

Tell about it: Tell what you know about extinct and endangered animals.

Find out: Would a baby whale fit in your classroom or living room? If a 100 foot whale was lying on the playground or your sidewalk, where would it's head be? It's tail? Have someone help you measure.

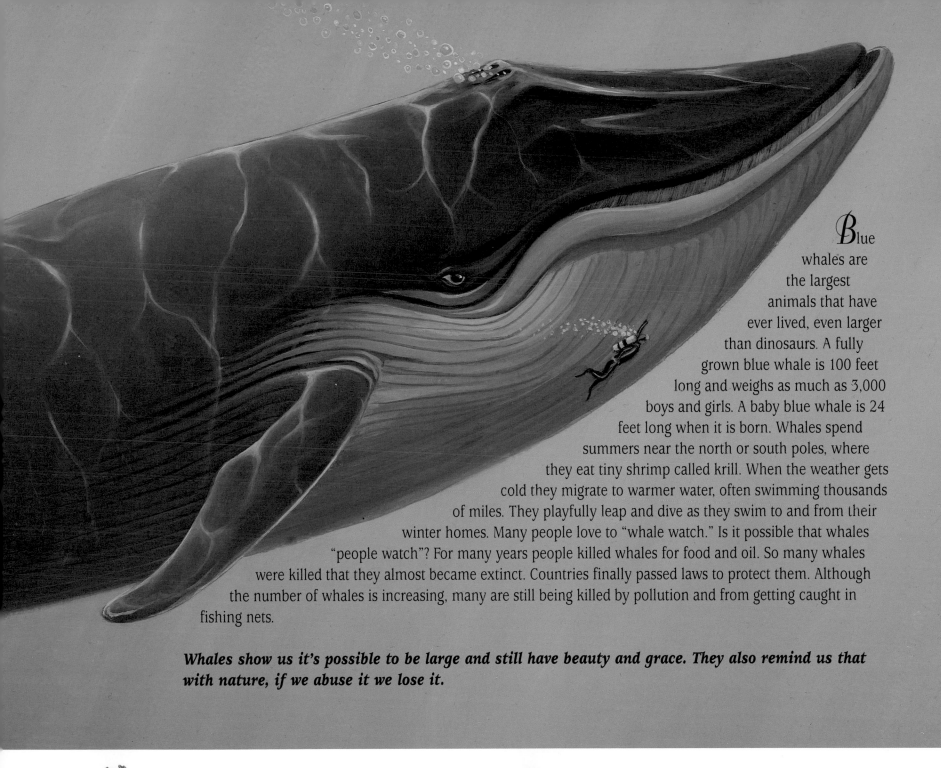

$\mathcal{B}$lue whales are the largest animals that have ever lived, even larger than dinosaurs. A fully grown blue whale is 100 feet long and weighs as much as 3,000 boys and girls. A baby blue whale is 24 feet long when it is born. Whales spend summers near the north or south poles, where they eat tiny shrimp called krill. When the weather gets cold they migrate to warmer water, often swimming thousands of miles. They playfully leap and dive as they swim to and from their winter homes. Many people love to "whale watch." Is it possible that whales "people watch"? For many years people killed whales for food and oil. So many whales were killed that they almost became extinct. Countries finally passed laws to protect them. Although the number of whales is increasing, many are still being killed by pollution and from getting caught in fishing nets.

Whales show us it's possible to be large and still have beauty and grace. They also remind us that with nature, if we abuse it we lose it.

Think about it: If someone told you they had "a whale of a good time" at your house, what do you think they mean?

Look it up: Many whales don't have teeth. They have baleen instead. Look up "whale" to find out what baleen is and what it looks like.

A lifetime for an **African crocodile** is about **50 years.**

*N*ile crocodiles are bothered by tiny animals that get on their skin and in their mouths. A bird called the Egyptian plover likes to eat these little animals. The crocodiles let the plovers land on their backs so they can eat the tiny pests. They even seem to open their mouths wider so the plovers, like over-eager dentists, can hop right in. The croc could easily get a quick lunch, but no one has ever seen a crocodile eat a plover.

Nile crocodiles remind us that everyone needs help from others sometimes.

Tell about it: Tell about a time when you really needed help and someone helped you.

Look it up: A crocodile is a reptile. What other animals are reptiles?

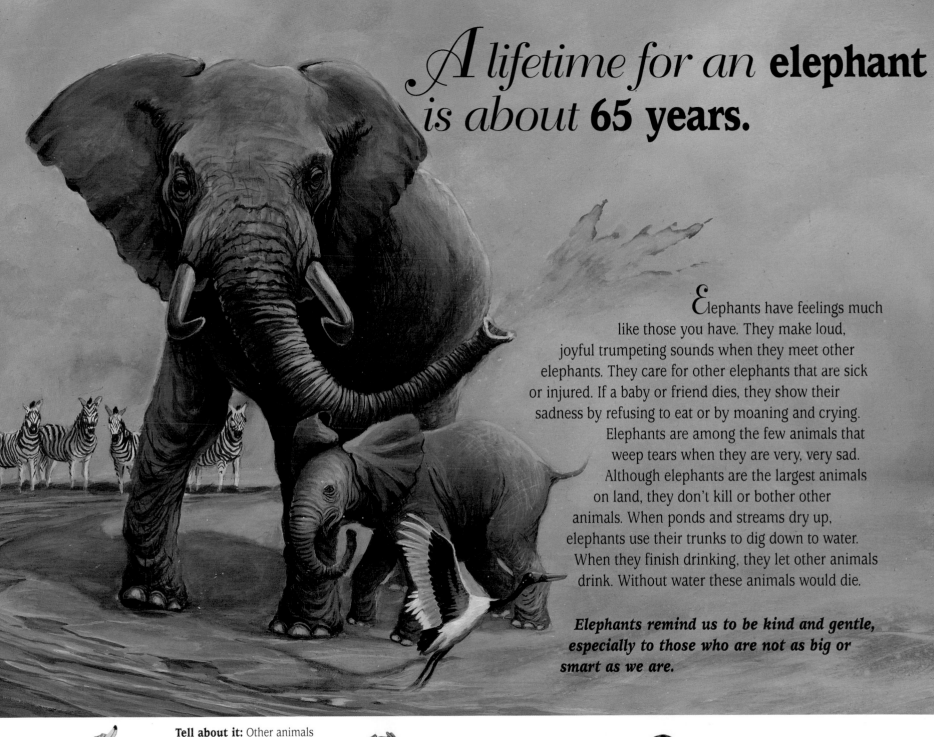

A lifetime for an **elephant** *is about* **65 years.**

Elephants have feelings much like those you have. They make loud, joyful trumpeting sounds when they meet other elephants. They care for other elephants that are sick or injured. If a baby or friend dies, they show their sadness by refusing to eat or by moaning and crying. Elephants are among the few animals that weep tears when they are very, very sad. Although elephants are the largest animals on land, they don't kill or bother other animals. When ponds and streams dry up, elephants use their trunks to dig down to water. When they finish drinking, they let other animals drink. Without water these animals would die.

Elephants remind us to be kind and gentle, especially to those who are not as big or smart as we are.

Tell about it: Other animals also have feelings, much like people. Tell about a time when you saw an animal that showed caring, happiness or sadness.

Think about it: Do you think a spider, insect or lizard feels sad or lonely when kept in a jar or can?

Look it up: There are two kinds of elephants: African elephants and Indian elephants. Find out how they are different.

A lifetime for a **saguaro** cactus is about **100 years.**

*I*f water were money, the saguaro (sa-WAR-o) would be rich. The saguaro grows in the desert where it doesn't rain for eight or nine months at a time. The temperature can get as hot as 120° F. Most plants can't live in such a hot, dry place. But when it does rain, the saguaro saves as much as it can. It stores up to 250 gallons of water in its thick stem to keep it alive until the next rain. Where most plants can't grow at all, the saguaro thrives and grows up to 60 feet tall. The saguaro shares its wealth. Many desert animals depend on the saguaro for food and moisture. Native Americans who live in the desert use its juicy red fruit to make jam or syrup.

Saguaros teach us how important it is to save—and to share.

Tell about it: Tell about a time when you planned for the future by saving money to buy something.

Find out: Is the saguaro cactus taller than a telephone pole? Find a pole and take 25 big steps away from it. That's about 60 feet. If the pole fell down, would the top reach you?

Look it up: Saguaro National Monument is a national park in the desert. It has a lot of saguaros. Find out where it is located.

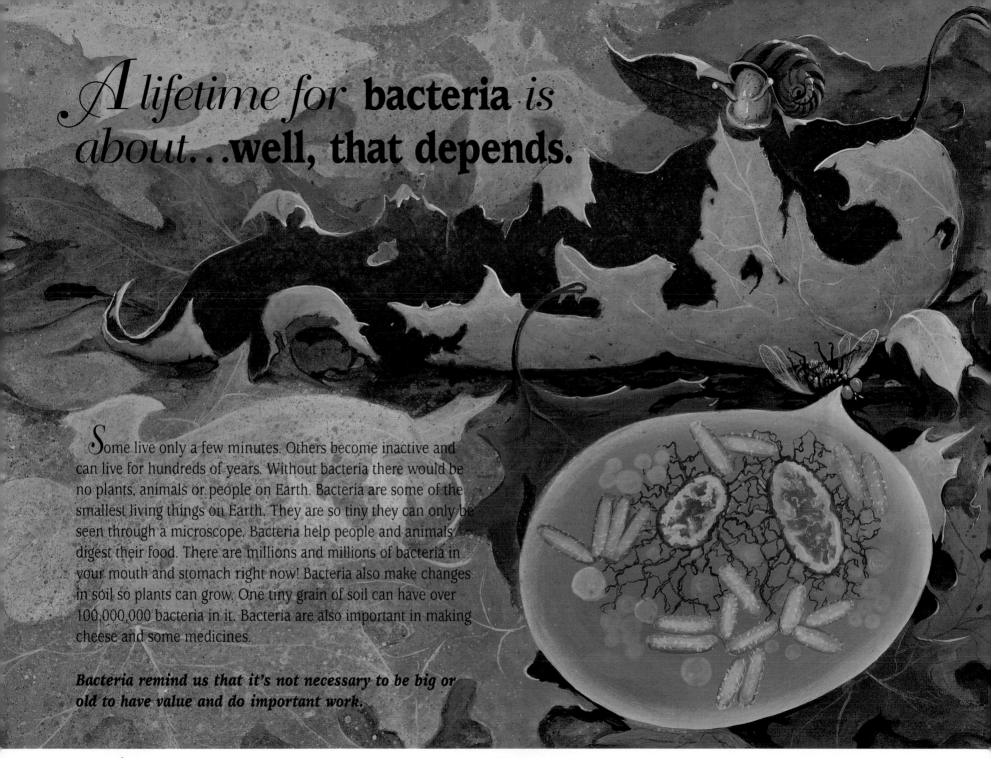

A lifetime for **bacteria** *is about…* **well, that depends.**

Some live only a few minutes. Others become inactive and can live for hundreds of years. Without bacteria there would be no plants, animals or people on Earth. Bacteria are some of the smallest living things on Earth. They are so tiny they can only be seen through a microscope. Bacteria help people and animals digest their food. There are millions and millions of bacteria in your mouth and stomach right now! Bacteria also make changes in soil so plants can grow. One tiny grain of soil can have over 100,000,000 bacteria in it. Bacteria are also important in making cheese and some medicines.

Bacteria remind us that it's not necessary to be big or old to have value and do important work.

Tell about it: Tell about some things you have done that you feel were important.

Find out: Some bacteria make people sick. Pink eye, strep throat and ear infections are all caused by bacteria. Find out if you have ever had any of these illnesses.

A lifetime for a **giant sequoia** is about **2,000 years.**

Giant sequoias are the largest living things on Earth, and one of the oldest. The General Sherman tree in Sequoia National Park is over 270 feet tall and 36 feet across. It weighs as much as 2,000 cars and is as tall as a 25 story building. People come from all over the world to visit the sequoia groves and stand beneath the peaceful, towering giants. Gazing up at these mighty beings, so ancient and magnificent, is an experience unlike any other. Many of today's "big trees" were hundreds of years old when Jesus was born, and ancient before Europeans came to America.

Sequoias show us how magnificent nature was, is, and always will be.

 Tell about it: Tell about a time when you were among trees, and felt particularly peaceful and happy.

 Find out: If everyone in your class held hands and made a circle, would the circle be big enough to go around the General Sherman tree? Is your circle 36 feet across or more?

 Look it up: Sequoias used to grow all over the United States and Canada. Now they grow in only one state. Which one? About how many ancient sequoia groves are left?

A lifetime for a **banyan tree** is about...
well, no one knows!

*B*anyan trees grow in an unusual way. A bird drops a seed in the branches of a palm or other tree. The seed grows roots that hang down until they reach the ground. The hanging roots then become the tree trunk, and branches grow. These branches put down new trunks. These trunks grow new branches that put down new trunks. They just keep growing and growing. Banyan trees can have over 350 main trunks and over 3,000 smaller trunks. Several thousand people can stand in their shade at the same time. No one knows how long a banyan tree can live.

Banyan trees show us that we don't have to do things the way everyone else does them.

Tell about it: Tell about a time when you did something a different way than others do it.

Find out: Many banyan trees grow in India. Can you find India on a map of the world?

A lifetime for a **dinosaur** *is…* **never again!**

*F*or 125 million years dinosaurs roamed the face of the Earth. Then they became extinct. They just disappeared. The last dinosaurs lived until about 65 million years ago, long before there were people on Earth. Scientists aren't sure why the dinosaurs all died. Some think the weather changed, causing the plants they ate to die. Other scientists believe a six mile wide rock, called an asteroid, hit the Earth causing fires and a worldwide cloud of dust, smoke and vapor that for several months blocked sunlight from reaching the Earth. A lack of sunlight might cause thousands of plants and animals, including dinosaurs, to become extinct. We'll probably never know what really happened.

Dinosaurs remind us that life doesn't last forever, and that we should appreciate and enjoy each day as we go along.

 **Tell about it:** Tell about some of the things in your life that you appreciate and enjoy each day as life goes along.

 Think about it: Is it possible that millions of years ago a dinosaur stood exactly where you are right now?

 Look it up: Since people have never seen a dinosaur, how do we know what they looked like, what they ate, and how they lived?

Scientists think the lifetime of **Earth** *up to now is about* **four and a half billion years.**

Earth is often called "Mother Earth" because it provides everything we need to live except light and heat. Mother Earth provides air to breathe, water to drink, and food to eat. She also provides a safe place for millions of different kinds of life to grow and develop. Dragonflies, for instance, have lived on the Earth for 250 million years. Sharks have been around for 300 million years.

Earth reminds us to be thankful to her and our mothers for the life they have given us.

 **Tell about it:** Tell about some things you have done that have helped the Earth. (For example: recycling newspapers, planting a tree, picking up trash in a park.)

 Find out: With an adult's help, put a white sock over the end of a car's exhaust pipe (be sure the pipe isn't hot). Have an adult run the car for five minutes. Without touching the hot pipe, remove the sock. You'll see five minutes of pollution from a slowly running car.

 Think about it: Earth has many problems, such as dirty air and water, too much garbage, and too many trees being cut down. How can you and your family help?

*Scientists think our **Sun** is about* **one hundred million years older than Earth.**

*I*t is one of millions and millions of stars in the Universe. The Sun provides the Earth with energy, both as light and heat. Without this energy from the Sun there could be no life on Earth. The Sun's energy spreads in all directions and reaches all of the planets and moons that move around it. But as far as we have discovered, only Earth has just the right conditions for people to exist. If we call Earth "Mother," should we call the Sun "Father"?

The Sun reminds us to let our energy shine out to others.

 **Tell about it:** Tell about a time when you especially appreciated the light or heat from the Sun.

 Think about it: There are millions, and probably billions of stars similar to our Sun. Do you think that any of these stars might have planets with life on them?

 Look it up: The Earth is about 92 million miles from the Sun. If the Sun stopped shining, how long would it be before the Earth would be in darkness? Look up "Sun" in the encyclopedia to find out.

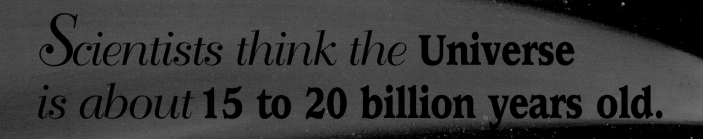

Scientists think the **Universe** is about **15 to 20 billion years old.**

The Universe is so big no one knows where it begins or where it ends. And it's getting bigger all the time. Scientists aren't sure how the Universe started or how long it will live. Some think it will live forever. Others believe that it will end but not for billions of years. People at all times and places have wondered how the Universe began, and why.

The vast Universe with its many mysteries reminds us that we don't know or understand nearly as much as we sometimes think we do.

Tell about it: Tell about how you feel when you look up in the sky at night and see uncountable numbers of stars.

Think about it: Where did the Universe come from?

Look it up: What did people long ago think the Moon, Sun and stars were? One place to look is in an encyclopedia under "Universe."

A lifetime for a **boy or girl** is about **85 years.**

 **Tell about it:** Tell about something you have done that is different from anything anyone ever did before. Maybe it's a picture you drew, a story you wrote, an idea you had, or a way you helped someone.

 Think about it: Is there another boy or girl who thinks just like you? Looks just like you? Has a name the same as yours?

You are one of the most creative living things on Earth. You have the ability to take information and ideas and use them to imagine new ideas. You also have the ability to be one of the most loving and caring creatures on Earth. By combining your ability to create with your ability to care, you can help make this "Spaceship Earth" a better place for all its passengers.

Your life is important. You have a special purpose on Earth.

No matter how short, no matter how long,
No matter how big, how smart or how strong,
All life has a place, a purpose, and worth,
All life is important on our planet Earth.

Look it up: How are humans different from apes? An encyclopedia will tell, under "human beings."

About the Author

David L. Rice's early years on a small farm near Fresno, California, formed the foundation for his lifelong appreciation of the interdependency of all life. While attending Pepperdine University in Los Angeles, his exposure to Native American culture and its respect and reverence for all of nature had a profound and lasting influence on him. David's career as a teacher of elementary and special education students provided many opportunities to share his love and appreciation of nature. Now that he is retired, he continues to work with children as a visiting author.

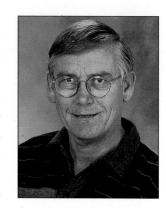

About the Illustrator

Michael S. Maydak spent much of his youth exploring the beautiful country of northern California. His appreciation for wildlife and the outdoors provides the inspiration for his artwork. An art graduate of San Jose State University, he has been a professional artist since 1976. He works in a studio at his home in Cool, California, where he lives with his wife and two children. He enjoys sharing his love of illustration with children.

Also available from Dawn Publications

A Teacher's Guide to Lifetimes by Bruce and Carol Malnor. Prepared by an experienced educator team, this guide offers a practical way for creative elementary teachers to incorporate *Lifetimes* into the science and language arts curriculum. Each lesson plan is clearly presented, including its objective, the relevant skill for living, and educational benchmark. Each activity is based on the principles of flow learning and brain compatibility to maximize student interest and learning retention. To order please call 800-545-7475.

Dawn Publications is dedicated to inspiring in children a deeper understanding and appreciation for all life on Earth. To order, to obtain a catalog, or for information about school visits by our authors and illustrators, please consult our website, www.DawnPub.com or call 800-545-7475.